RECENT PAINTINGS BY ANTHONY BARTON

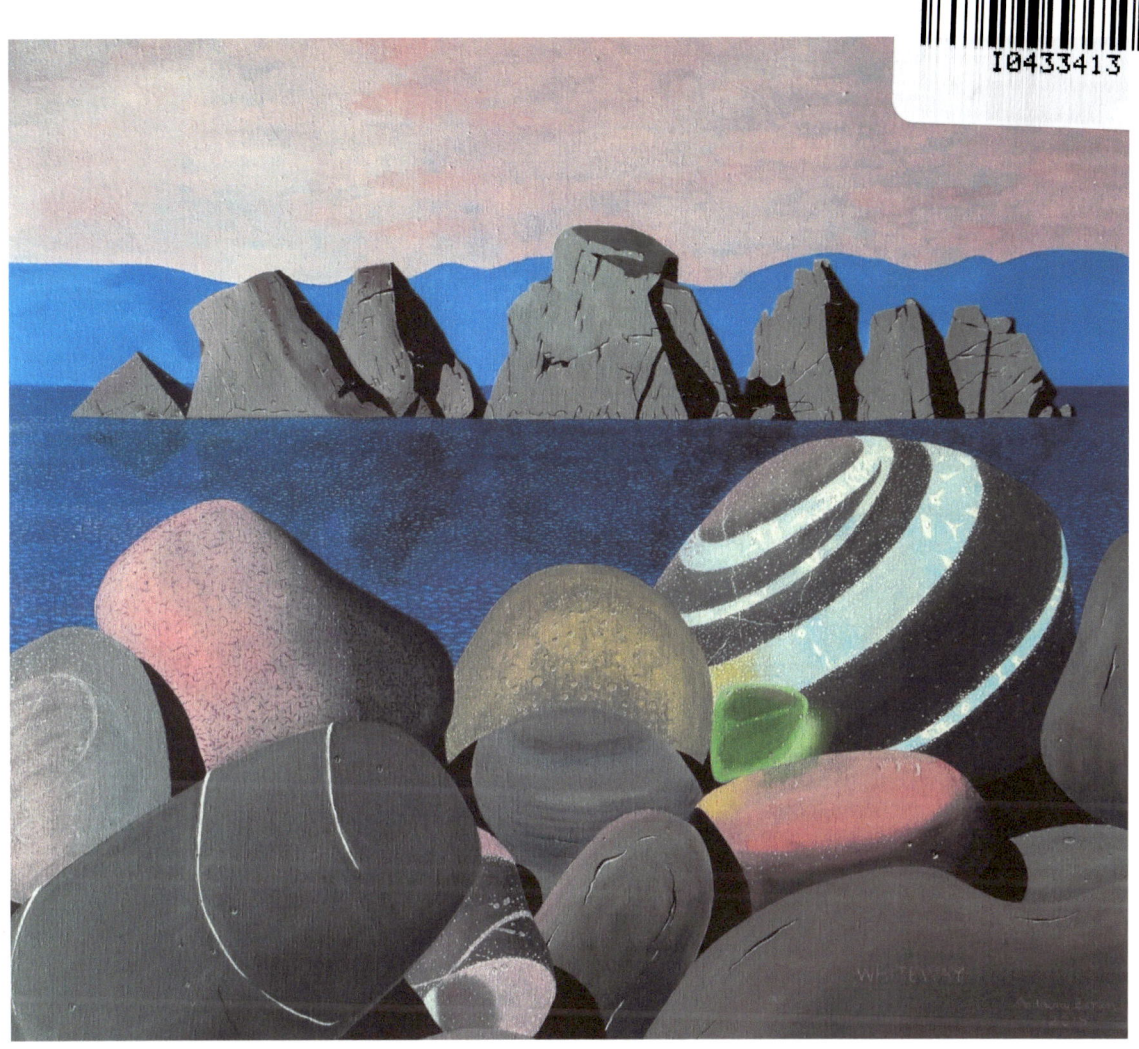

'WHITEWAY' BY ANTHONY BARTON 2015 OILS ON CANVAS 32" X 37"
PURCHASED BY THE PROVINCIAL ART BANK FOR THE ROOMS

PREFACE

My late friend Philip Hicks (1921-2017) once served as the art critic for the *Evening Telegram*. He came to interview me in my studio at Perry's Cove on the occasion of an exhibition of my work being held at the Annex Gallery in Bond Street in 1987, and had this to say:

Anthony Barton's technique is a straightforward one – unpretentious, without the posturing so prevalent in much Art-art today. He paints because he is right into his subject matter, and when he refers to "the whole planet being a living organism" and to the interrelatedness of all life, you become aware immediately of this element in his painting.

Such an outlook can only give his art an intensity and significance of its own, and when combined with an original and enquiring mind, an individual way of looking at things, and a background of travel and different experiences, it isn't surprising that his work has a content that is special to him.

What it is is impossible to describe in words. Art is its own explanation and a painter says it all, just as it is, on the canvas.'

In Anthony Barton's case, his painting is linked to his way of life. The large studio space in which we talked was bare except for a strip of red carpet on the floor, a table and a couple of chairs, an easel and the pictures on the walls. That is how he wants it. He doesn't have TV or radio, nor does he read the papers – not as an affectation, but for the freedom and directness that simplicity brings.

We walked down over the rocks to the shore and it was easy to see why the artist doesn't want to live anywhere else, and what it is that has taken hold. The elemental quality that appears in the rock, the movement of the sea, the water itself, the run of the cliffs and the land masses themselves, together with the light, the sky and the clouds – all these appear in a different form in his painting, not just as a representation, but as intense feeling.

I thank Philip for his encouragement, and present in these pages a handful of reproductions of a few of my most recent works as a way of remembering him. As I read Philip's words I hear his voice in my head. He was a true writer. He wrote as he spoke.

Anthony Barton, Perry's Cove, Newfoundland

1 August 2017

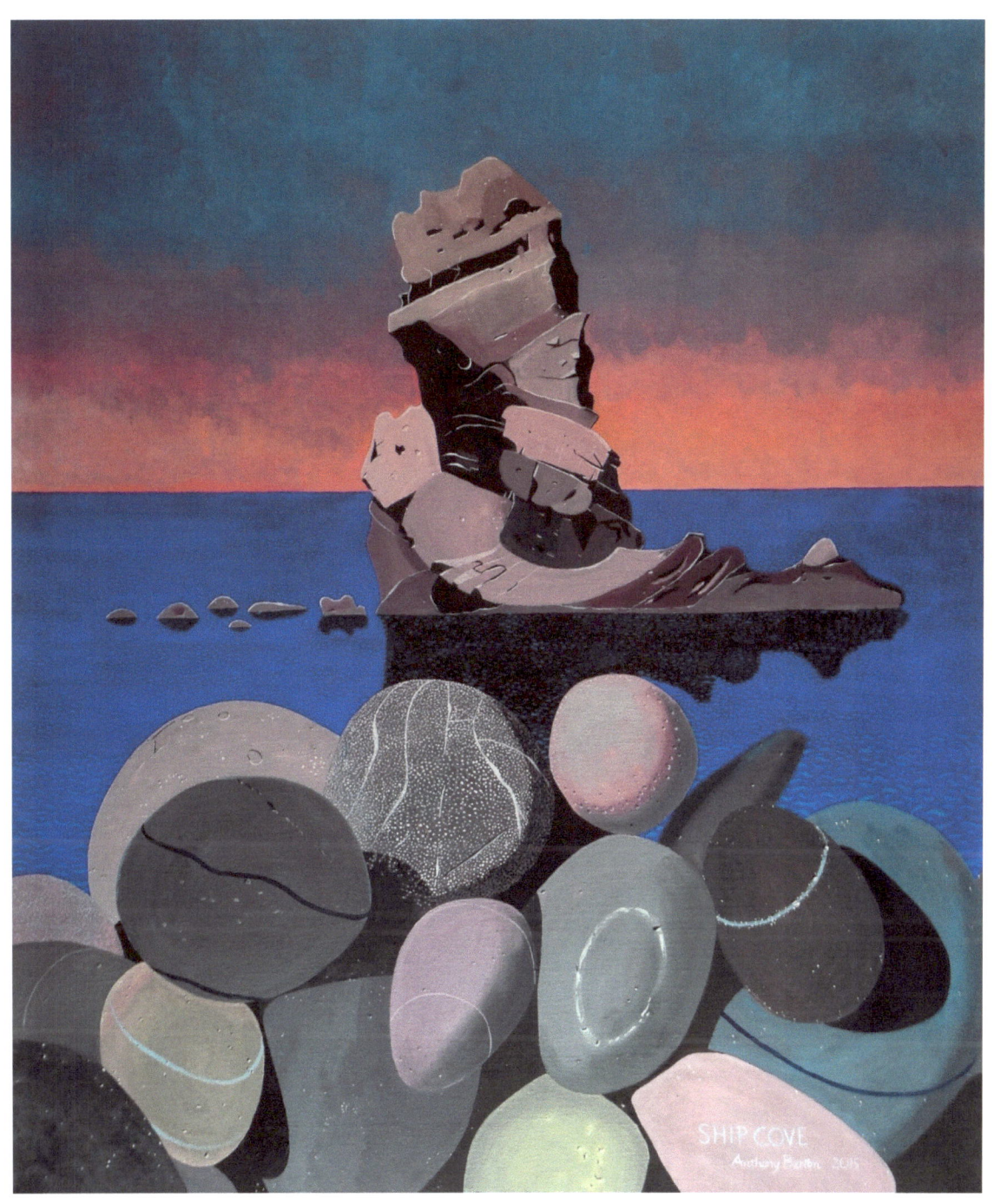

'SHIP COVE' BY ANTHONY BARTON 2015 OILS ON CANVAS 37" X 32"
COLLECTION OF WILLIAM AND MONICA BARRY

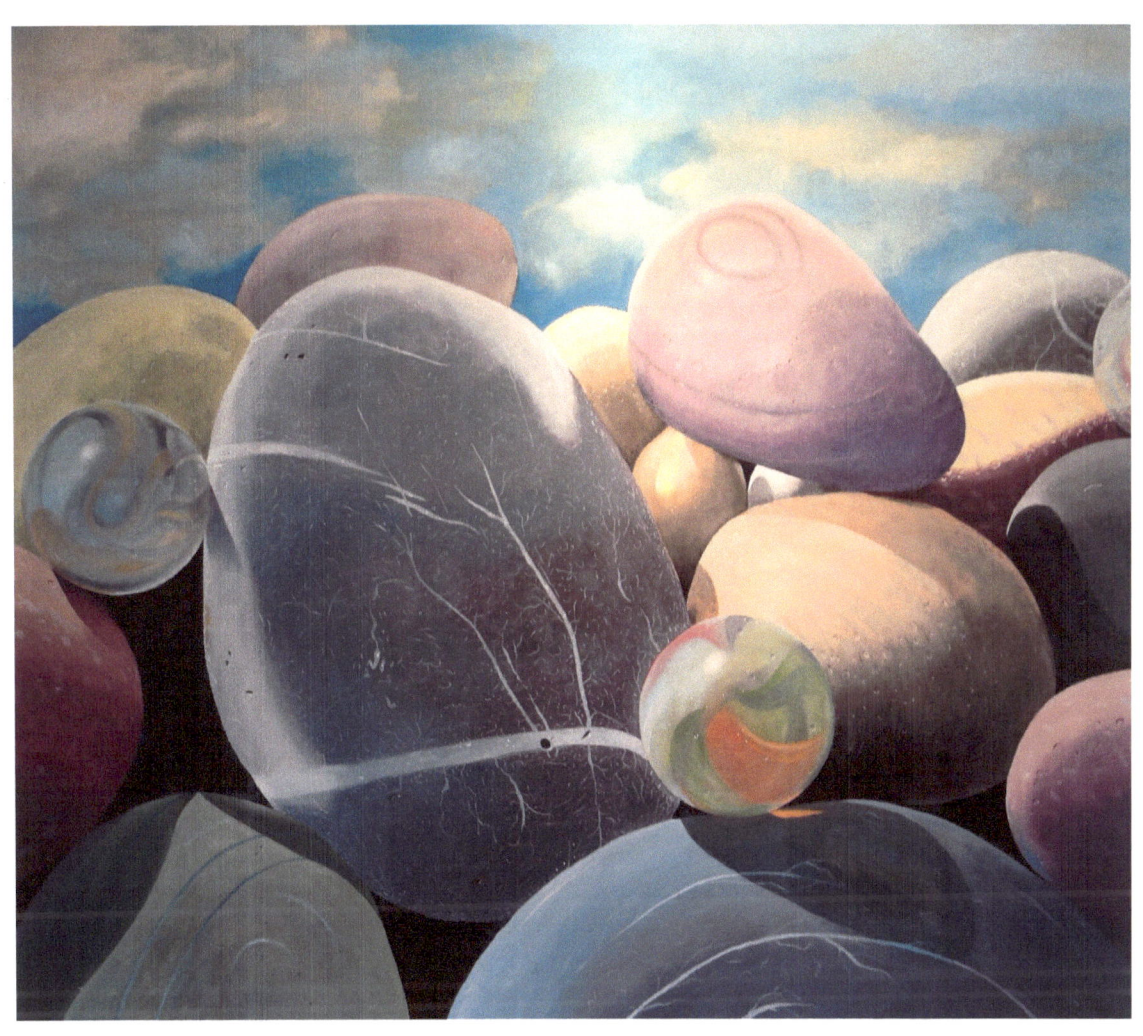

'SUNSET PEBBLES' BY ANTHONY BARTON 2016
OILS ON CANVAS 32" X 37"

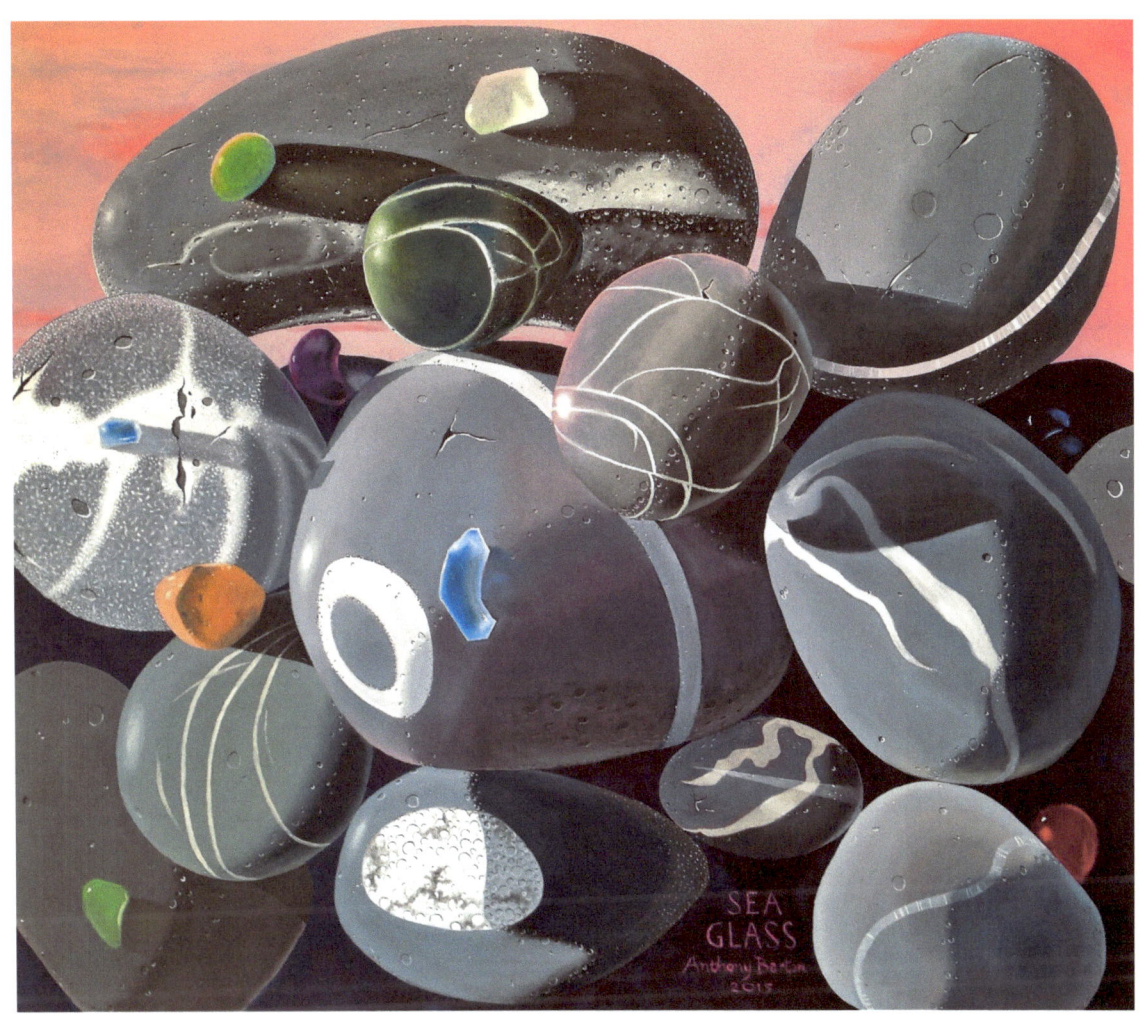

'SEA GLASS' BY ANTHONY BARTON 2015 OILS ON CANVAS 32" X 37"
PURCHASED AT AUCTION

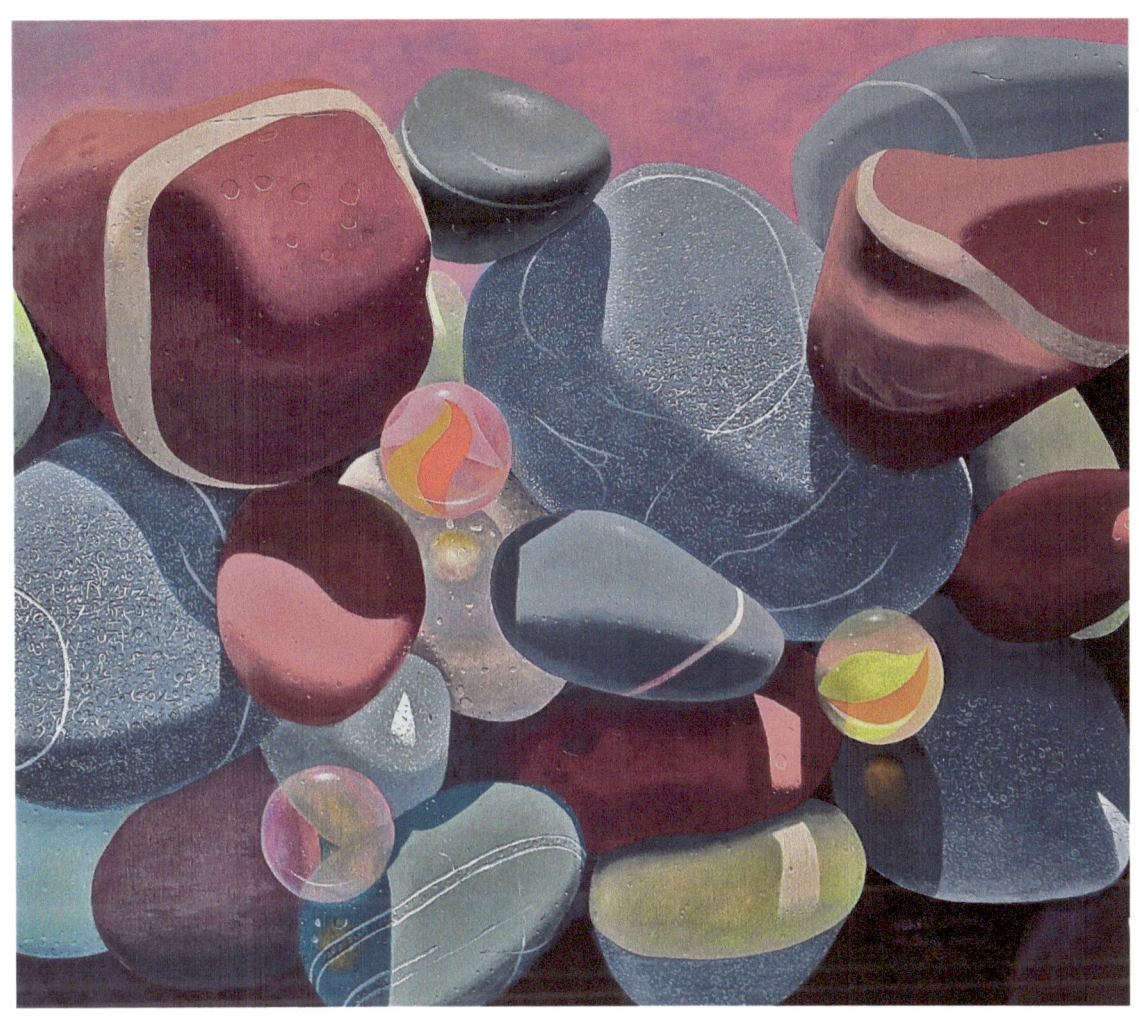

'SUNSET STONES' BY ANTHONY BARTON 2015
OILS ON CANVAS 32" X 37" SOLD BY THE EMMA BUTLER GALLERY

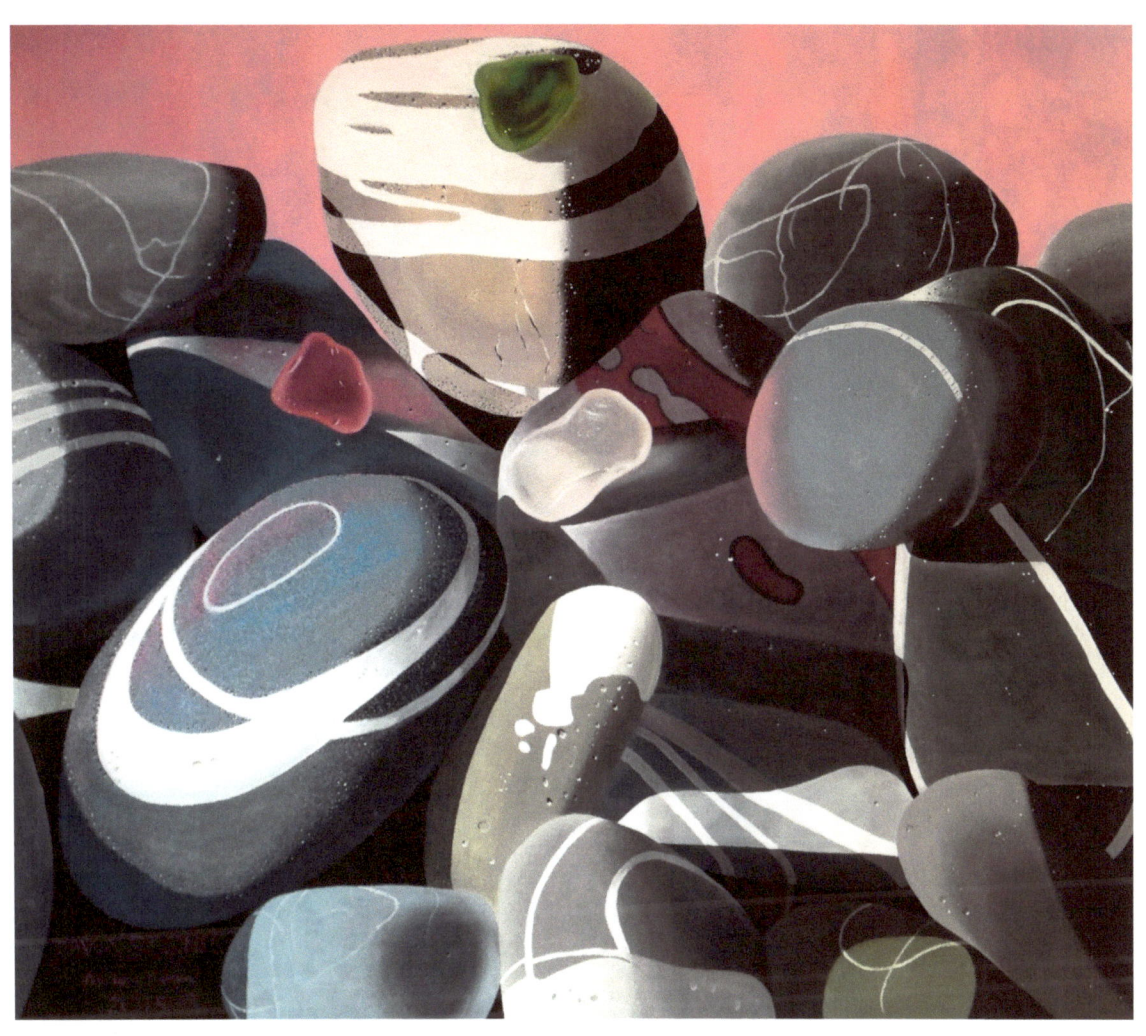

'DAWN STONES' BY ANTHONY BARTON 2015
OILS ON CANVAS 32" X 37" SOLD BY THE EMMA BUTLER GALLERY

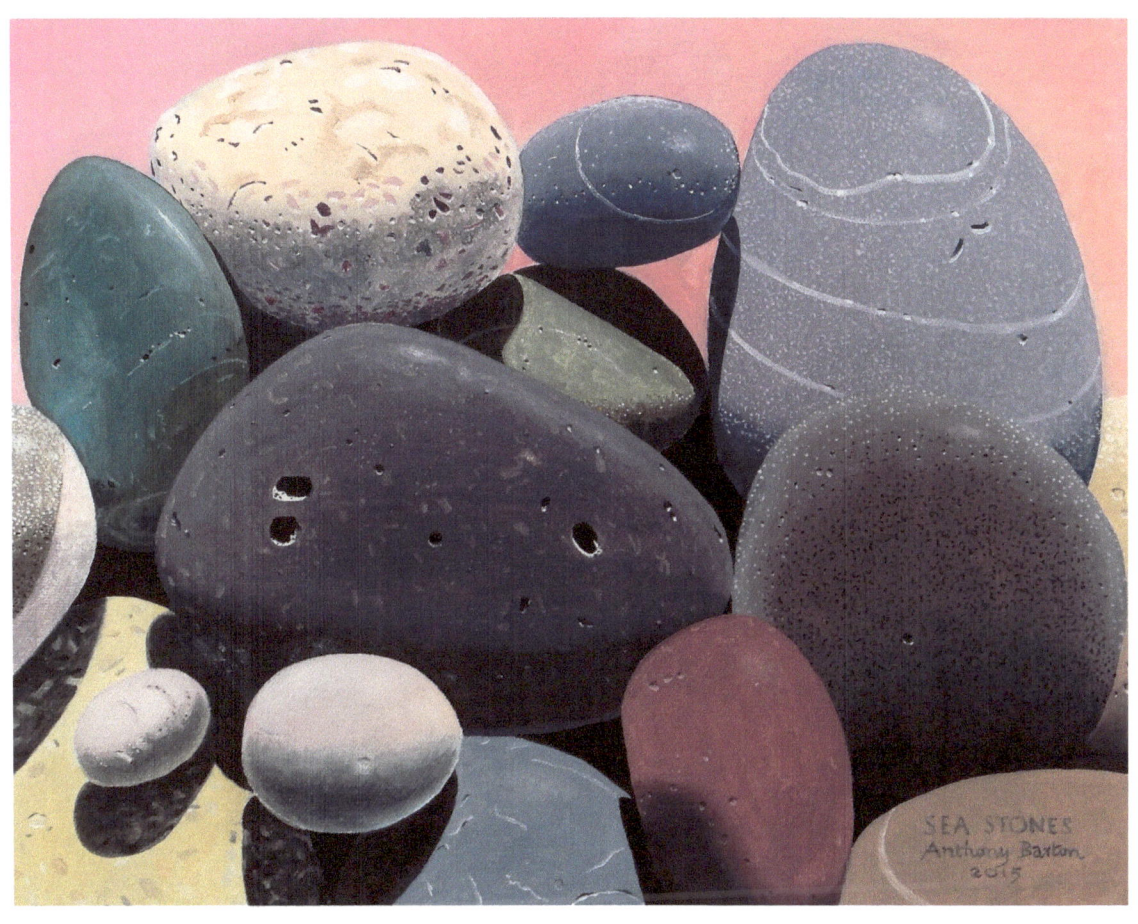

'SEA STONES' BY ANTHONY BARTON 2015 OILS ON CANVAS 11" X 14"
SOLD BY THE EMMA BUTLER GALLERY

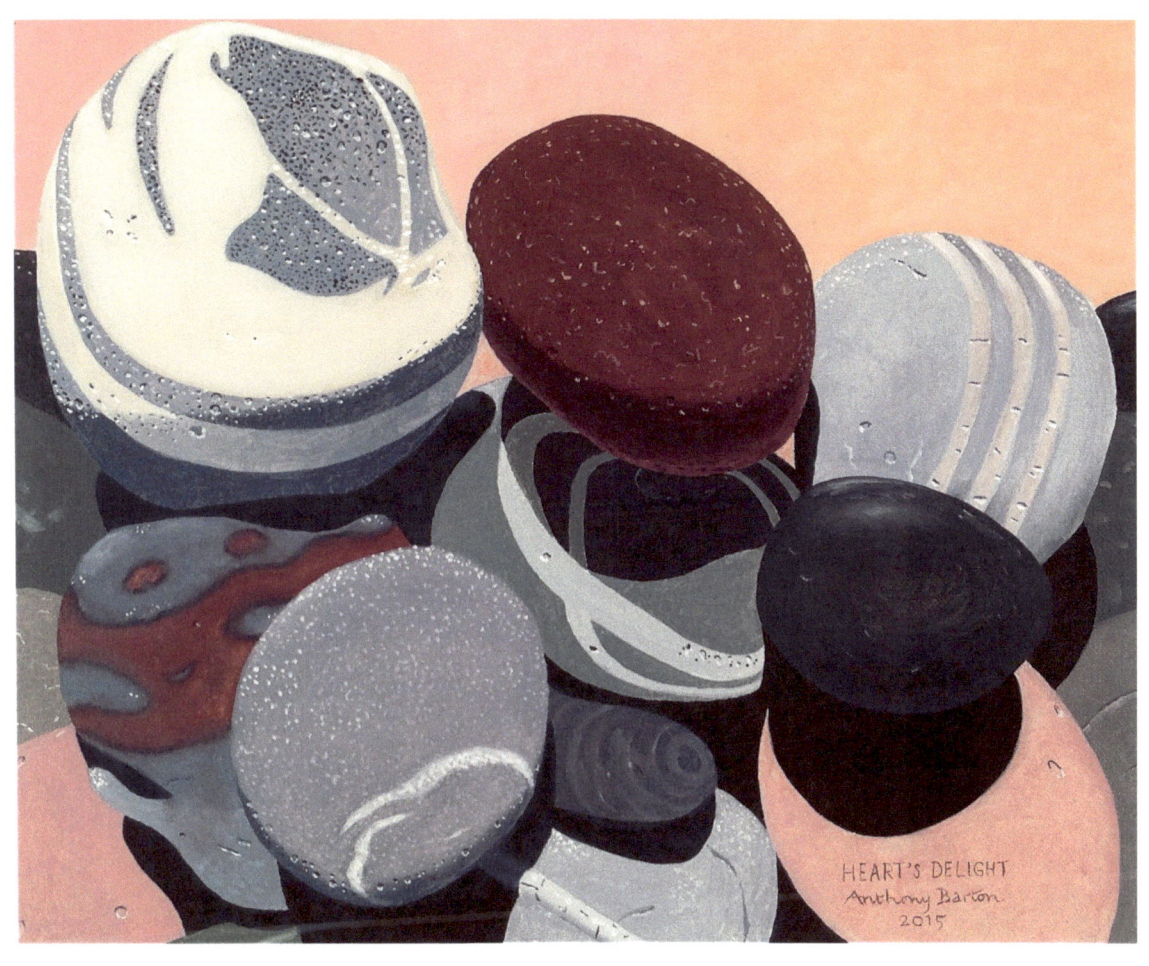

'HEART'S DELIGHT' BY ANTHONY BARTON 2015
OILS ON CANVAS 11" X 14" SOLD BY THE EMMA BUTLER GALLERY

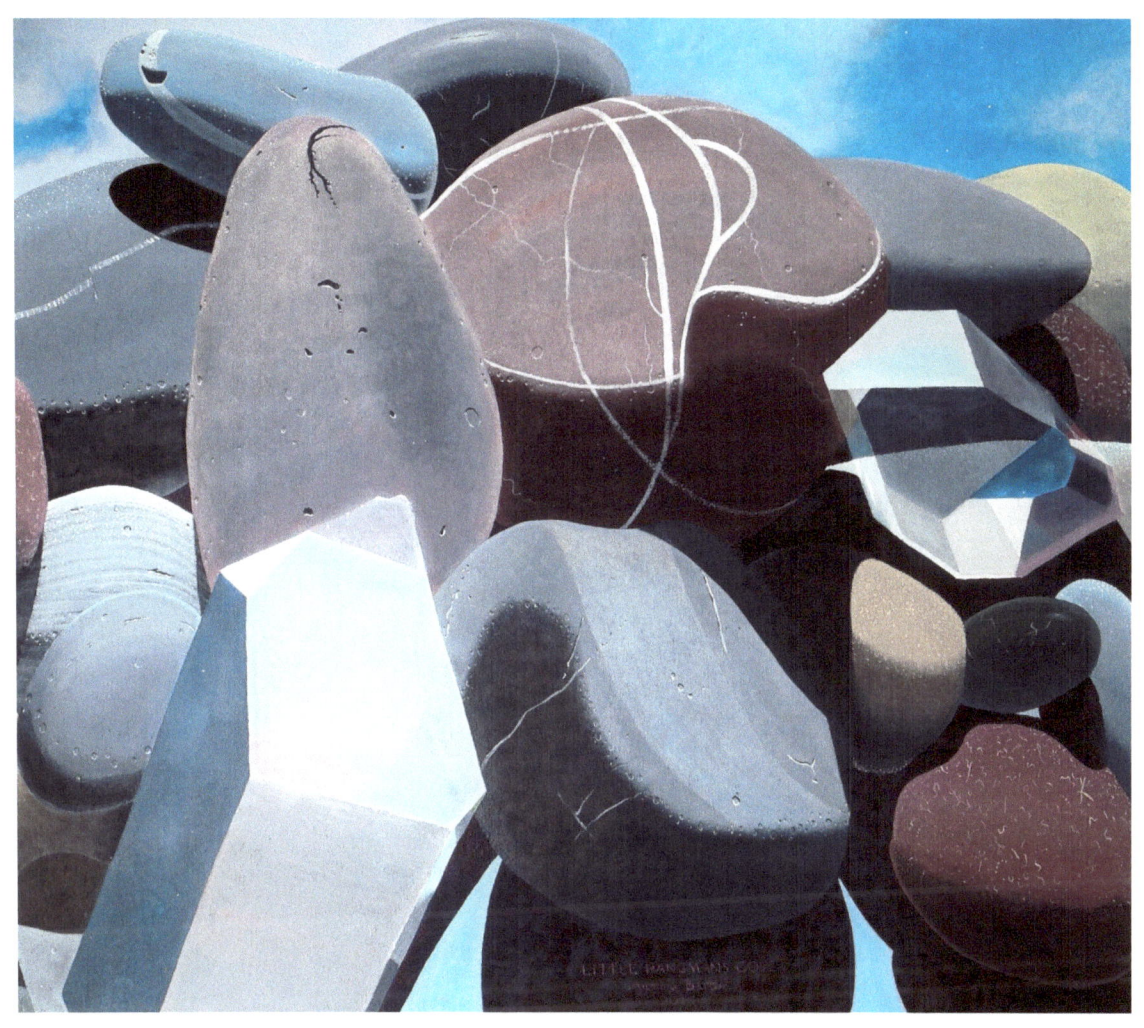

'LITTLE HANGMAN'S COVE' BY ANTHONY BARTON 2015 OILS ON CANVAS 32" X 37" COLLECTION OF MARIAN FRANCES WHITE

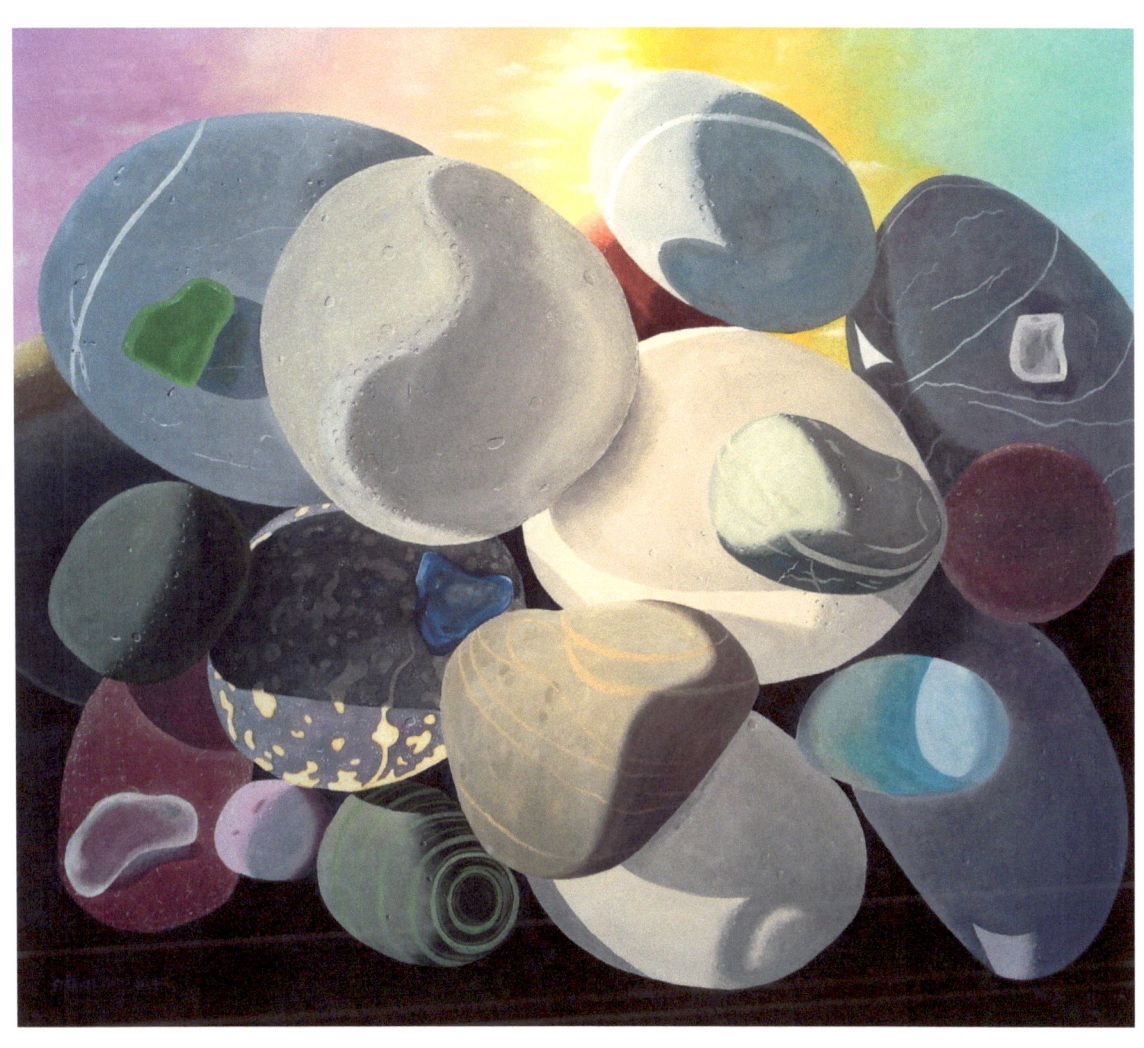

'DAWN PEBBLES' BY ANTHONY BARTON 2016
OILS ON CANVAS 32" X 37"

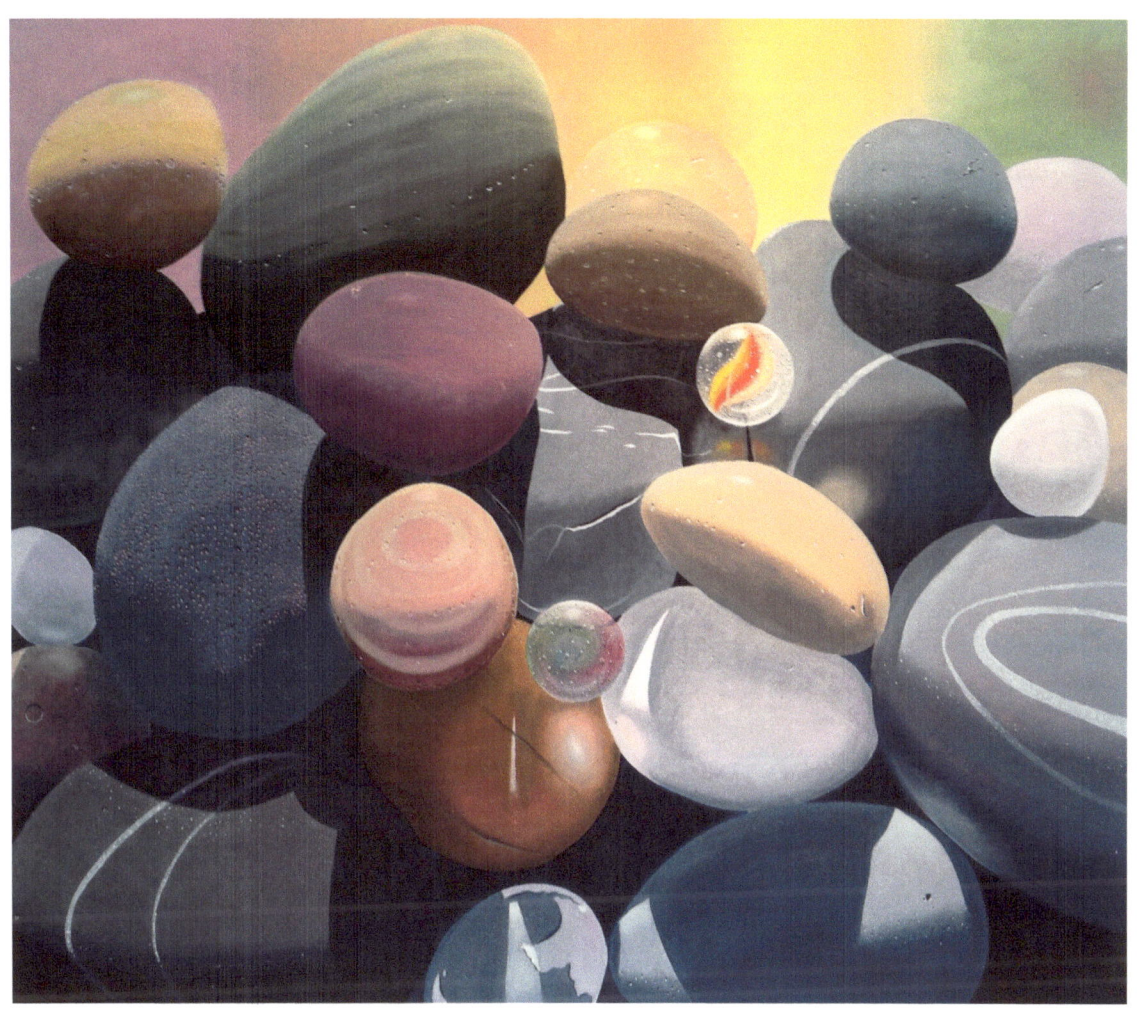

'COBBLE STONES' BY ANTHONY BARTON 2015
OILS ON CANVAS 32" X 37"

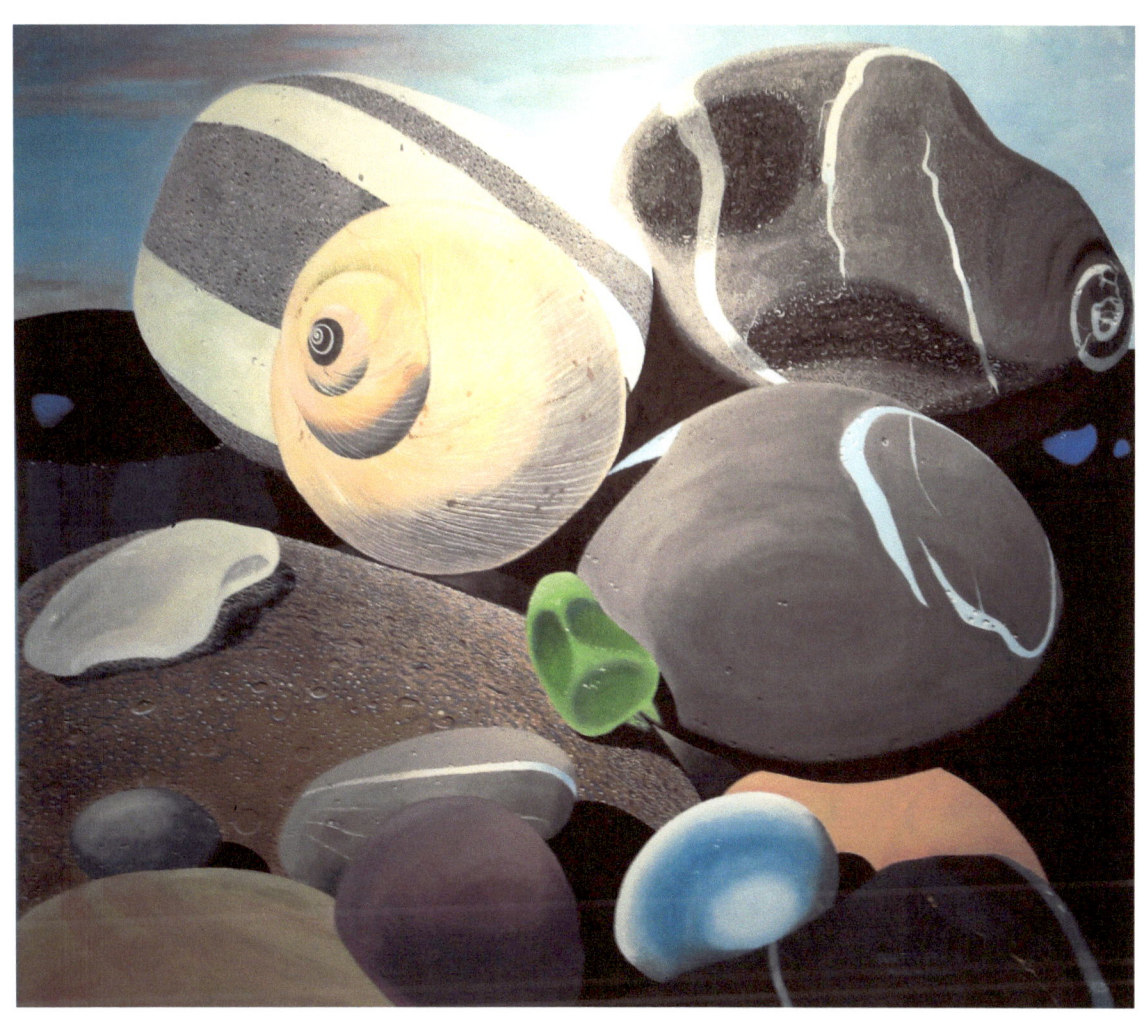

'WHITE'S BEACH' BY ANTHONY BARTON 2014
OILS ON CANVAS 32" X 37"

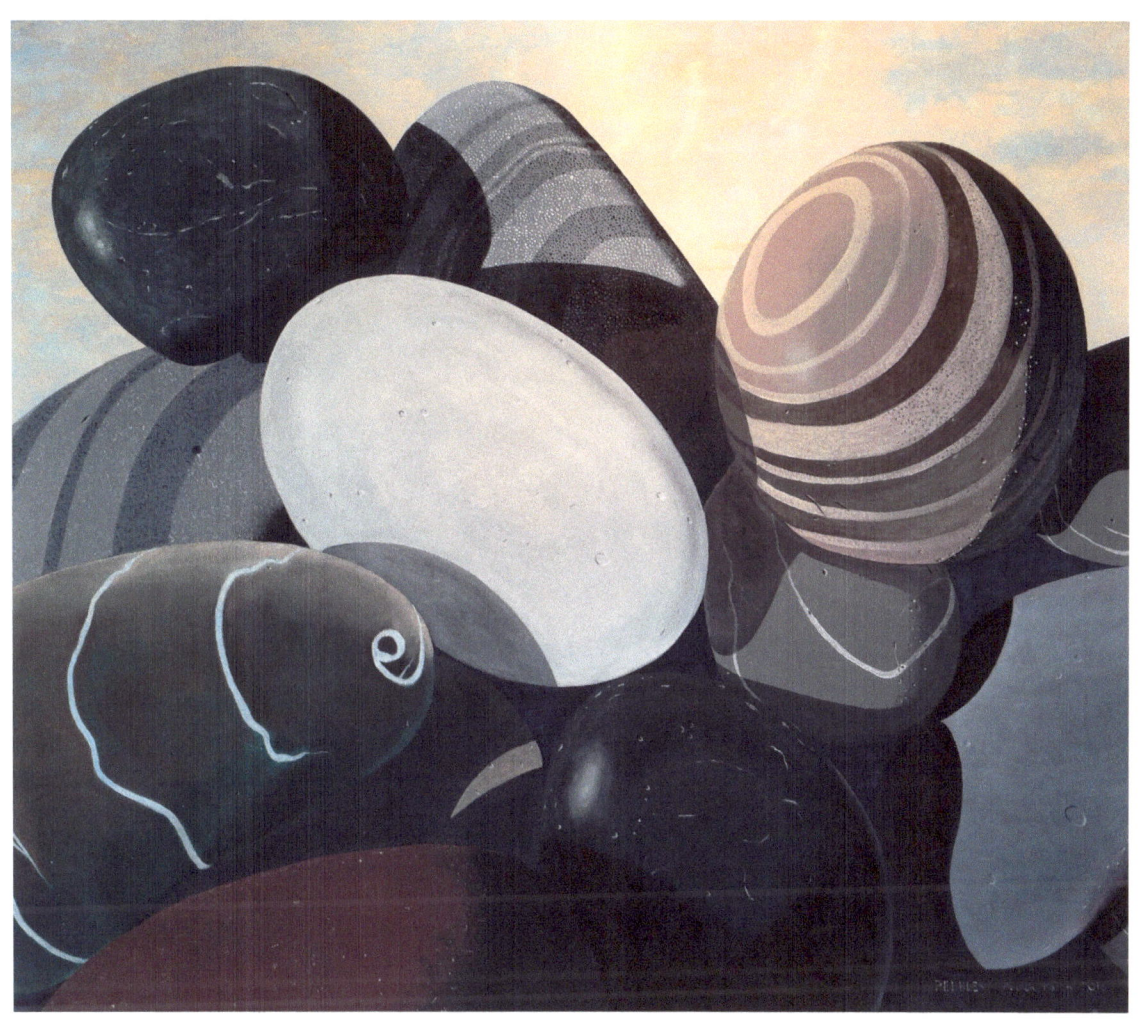

'PEBBLES' BY ANTHONY BARTON 2016
OILS ON CANVAS 32" X 37"

www.ingramcontent.com/pod-product-compliance
Lightning Source LLC
Chambersburg PA
CBHW051833210526
45473CB00005B/1862